THE LOST LETTERS

The Lost Letters

Catherine Greenwood

Brick Books

Library and Archives Canada Cataloguing in Publication

Greenwood, Catherine, 1960-, author
    The lost letters / Catherine Greenwood.

Poems.
ISBN 978-1-926829-85-2 (pbk.)

    1. Héloïse, 1101-1164--Poetry. 2. Abelard, Peter, 1079-1142--
Poetry. I. Title.

PS8613.R445L68 2013   C811'.6   C2013-904021-8

We acknowledge the Canada Council for the Arts, the Government of
Canada through the Canada Book Fund, and the Ontario Arts Council
for their support of our publishing program.

Canada Council   Conseil des Arts   Government   Gouvernement
for the Arts   du Canada   of Canada   du Canada

ONTARIO ARTS COUNCIL
CONSEIL DES ARTS DE L'ONTARIO

The author photo was taken by Jennifer Conklin.

This book is set in Minion Pro, designed by Robert Slimbach and
released in 1990 by Adobe Systems.

Design and layout by Cheryl Dipede.
Printed and bound by Sunville Printco Inc.

Brick Books
431 Boler Road, Box 20081
London, Ontario N6K 4G6
www.brickbooks.ca

for Steve

"At Last"…

✠

CONTENTS

IV
THE LOST LETTERS

✠

I

FROM THE HYMNAL

✠

And as most of these songs told of our love, they soon made me widely known and roused the envy of many women against me.
—Heloise to Abelard, *Letter 1*

✠

MONK LOVE BLUES

Got a little thing
I call the Monk Love Blues.
Heloise and Abelard –
this kinda thing ain't new.
See, when I say *monk*
I ain't talkin Thelonius.
The monk love I'm feelin
done verge on felonius.

      Yeah, I got them old Monk Love Blues.

I quake and quiver,
I shiver and pant
when I don't get my hit
of sweet Gregorian chant.
I'm jonesin for a fix
of my Brother man-in-black
(he ain't heavy, Honey,
just the Monk-ey on my back).

      Got chased by the Abbot
      for courtin a habit.
      I'm hooked on them Monk Love Blues.

I need an injection
of Holy Spirit,
but no matter how I try,
I can't get near it.
Flirt with him in Chapel,
he don't look my way,
if I walked up to him naked,
he'd just bow his head and pray.

      Got me the Monk Love Blues.

So I tried a little witchcraft
to make him mine,
slipped number-nine potion
in the Communion wine.
Well, it stirred up a commotion
in the rest of the Brethren,
but my Bro was immune,
didn't even need Confession.

       Feed him raw oyster?
       He heads for the Cloister.
       I'm stewin with the Monk Love Blues.

So I'll tell it to ya straight,
I ain't makin no bones,
Spirit's movin in me
like the Devil in Miss Jones.
Sometimes, you know, Babe,
we all have that urge.
How's about you lay it on me,
let me feel your scourge.

Come on Honey,
let me ring your bell.
Let me light your taper,
Let me wax your cell.
I wanna polish your Cross,
I'd get on my knees for you,
wait till Hell freezes over
just to warm your pew.

       Cause I got me the soul-sellin, Bible-humpin
       sweet, crazy Monk Love Blues.

O, Brother!

✠

II

TURTLE SOUP

✠

As if they knew that always beyond
and beyond the ladies were weaving them
into their spider looms.
—Phyllis Webb, "The Days of the Unicorns"

✠

TWO BLUE ELEPHANTS

Two elephants: blue as sky absorbed
in bodies of water, sorrow the marrow
of their spongy bones. Vessels of grief
so ancient they merely grin, blink salt

sweated through centuries of drought
from the glazed stones of their eyes,
raise trunks to scout moisture, shake
dirt from cracked hides and hoist themselves up,
huge sacks of tears on wrinkled knees.

From the sediment of a seabed
gone arid, they rise in a mist of dust
and wearily begin to batter a hatch
rusted shut, portal to the barnacled heart
of a hold filled with a fortune in sand dollars.

✠

Can you not feel the world
shudder and tremble, straining
against its hinges? We are lost as gods
who've lumbered into the wrong continent
and, without solace of worship, look down
to find our broad feet fashioned
into umbrella stands. How futile
the parasols we so foolishly open
against pain, as if joy were simple
as believing, like repelling sun or rain.

Here, I'm breaking this blue sleeping
tablet in two and sending you half,
that together we may fall
into a slumber and wake
on either side of the same dream.

Lord of Doorways,
accept our simple offering:
turquoise mirror in a mountain lake,
sesame cake baked with seed
stolen from the hidden cave,
mouse milk thinned with evaporated tears.

Open, let us in.

THE NATURAL HISTORY OF THE HAMSTER

after Milton Acorn

In her little corner of the endless
unthinkable desert, she bathes
in dewdrops. Guided at night
by a constellation
of seed piles, she keeps her short-
sighted eyes to the ground.

Eeny-meany-est of misanthropes,
she goes underground
by day, avoiding others of her kind
except for the obligatory two-second fling
(on film a hectic blur of fur)
a couple of times a year.

Acquisitive by nature, she
is crammed with miniscule worries,
briefcase cheeks stuffed full. In dreams
her bean-sized brain sends tendrils
heavenward and she plucks giant
pods from the sun's flower.

A minimalist, without stuttering
she utters her one-word poems – *kernel,*
liquid, snooze – just once
before scratching them in the sand
in a delicate script read only by rain
erasing her small hand.

LIZARD

Likes to think he knows
how to let go, when to leave
it all behind – that thing
the fat white grubs blindly investigate,

for instance, lying by the marigolds
beneath the bedroom window,
tied to a length of string
like a scaly grey finger.

He's given *it* the slip. And the girl
who tethered him there like some
cold-blooded puppy, he's left her
a token. Unaware that he bleeds

a sticky pink sap, he muses:
If you love something, set it free
and, blinking, trudges off broken,
his nether-end a slow dripping tap.

⁜

When the glistening stub
seals over, healed
like a fingertip erased of prints,
he can feel it begin to grow

backwards despite his forward
propulsion. As if form were
the index of being, this cell-by-cell
compulsion points toward

the past – trapped in it, no way
to make a clean break. The body,
seeking the faint trail of matter
spattered in the dust, insists upon

its own method of remembering.
He smells the blood he shed
back in that garden still. In his mind
the tail sprouts a brand new head.

MULE (BLACK-TAILED) DEER

Silver wraiths blurred by snow,
legs slender as twigs. In a fallen forest

they detach themselves from charred trunks
and listen. Their ears, black-tinged brooms,

sweep the singed air. Smudged muzzles
glisten where they have sipped pure

thought from the streams, chill clarity
the mind dips into then shakes off –

a drizzle of ink from a calligrapher's
brush. Flicking blunt tails,

they fade among somnolent birch,
disappearing into the edge where pines hide

snow-blind heads in the bristled sky.
Sharp hooves puncture the skin of drift

with tracks, each empty black dot
aligned with the bright illusion

winter has embroidered on the speckled pelt
of the fawn. Each transitory knot stitching up

a white story the mule deer smuggle
deeper into the season's dormant

soul. Within every silent bearer –
winter's narcotic cold, the coming melt.

SILVER-HAIRED BAT
CAUGHT IN A CEILING LAMP

Following twilight
appetites, he swallowed
unthinking the aphrodisiac
rumour of moths.

Conducting an inquiry
into brightness, he saw
the light and followed
their sputtering flight

over the lamp's smooth lip,
seduced by what drew
those unblinking orbs
charcoaled on their wings.

Now the world's outside
in, hunger become entrapment.
Still blind, he smells
sizzled flutter, singed fur.

Struggling to climb out
he slips on walls
the shape of an upturned bell,
his body an ashen clapper.

☩

And what of us
headed upstairs to bed expecting
nothing but summer air
to enter the open window?

The sight of a dark
silhouette projected
against the opaque white
globe – a hundred watts

baking him like a chick
in an incubator, Hell's
hatchling – provokes horror
and pity. A stepladder!

How many sets of hands
does it take to open hope, unscrew
the lid tightened on that jar
of misguided longings?

☦

Tipped from the lamp
out he spills on the sill,
still as a lump of silvery coal
dumped from a scuttle.

Black cloak collapsed, bones
poke beneath the membrane
of his skin like spokes
of a broken umbrella.

Above the lawn mosquitoes hum.
He unfolds webbed fingers,
his singular pair of wings.
Singing, re-enters the night.

FAITH

My cat watches the wall for hours, waiting for the light
     to emerge from its den of shadow.
She lures it with a confusion of bird calls,
     imitating the unheard
voice of her prey. To what does silence respond?
I tuck the flashlight in my sleeve, turn it on.
The beam flies to the ceiling, flickers wall to floor,
     cat leaping after
this luminous bird-snake of dust mote,
     this weightless nothing
sliding from her claws without sound, slipping away
     scentless.

No fool, she knows whose game she plays.
     I pick up the flashlight and
her ears flick back at the snick of the switch.
I'm a snake-oil peddler, back-road revivalist pitching
     visions on tent walls,
but she doesn't care. Her fervent calls charm
     the shine from up my sleeve.
She suspends disbelief, stalks the light, paws
     slicing through it
in the radiant air. Like any human, swayed
     by the apparition
of an unnamed species of miracle.

MERMAID APPEAL

Nereid conductress,
your song is more ghostly
than the long-forgotten lowing of sea cows
herded through gunsight to extinction;

shy sea nun,
your undulant jade tail outglimmers
the forked legs of your sisters who renounce
their oyster-shell bras and the salt cloister for land;

siren, seductress,
your body of watery lore
outweighs the aquarium's corpulent dugong
agraze in her paddock of placid green silence –

in your legendary mirror show me
myself, the true, elusive face of one

who never learned to wear a skirt.

IF LIFE HANDS YOU TURTLES,
MAKE TURTLE SOUP

Having dredged themselves
out of the mud, the turtles lie
sunning themselves on a log.
Army helmets from an old battle. The smallest,
size of a hand grenade, little pinhead
tucked in, basks on a reedy hummock.

As a kid I kept a pet turtle in a compound
with a tiny plastic palm. One morning
my mother tried rinsing him under the tap
but he wouldn't wake up, so we buried him
in the flower bed. I've learned since that
turtles hibernate, and now live with the guilty
notion we buried Timmy alive. But perhaps
he escaped and that's him out on the log,
like some deposed dictator resurfacing
in southern California to operate
hair-replacement salons.

Which is why, to help us
keep these guys straight, every war
needs a trademark:
Don't Go Home with Your Hard-On.
Awe, Shocks!
Slow and Steady Wins the Race.

BUSHTIT'S NEST

[T]heir flitterings were an attempt to summon
something out of nothing...
—Don McKay, *Vis à Vis*

on a branch of the Indian Plum
hangs a sock in the rain

a thick wet sock knitted from twigs
and unruly ear hair of elderly men
gritty green clam beards festooned
with small rocks   tangled blown
combings from a neighbourhood cat
named Hunter   rat whiskers
broom straw   corn silk
culled from the compost box
thread from unravelling
edges of prayer flags

heavy as a clock's pendulum
it is weighted with
the rationed orange in the stocking
hung Christmas morning
at the foot of the bed that Betty shared
with her younger brothers the older ones
at sea   while in the dark scullery
their mother made rice pudding

inside it are decommissioned coins
including a genuine silver dollar

inside it are Gran's missing dentures
her eyeglasses   the hearing aid
lost by the orderlies   the letter Jack wrote her
when all those years ago
he ran off to India

on its sodden bough it sways
as swings the vein-woven scrotum
on the red bull plodding
down the dirt road toward Uncle Ted's
bellowing cows   his cock
a pink carrot pointing the way

WEB

A typical barbwire fence on wood posts surrounded
the field about six kilometres east of McBride....
[I]t looked like the whole area was covered with an
opaque, white plastic grocery store bag.
—CBC News, November 27, 2002

            no alcazars or office towers
parliament buildings shopping centers
pavilions minarets

the spiders have set up their looms
in the cow pasture
pitched gauzy white tents
on the fence posts

silken energies pour
like water from spinnerets
clear caramelized wires run out
from the spigots of being

above the frozen dung
of a few trodden acres of soil
they have chosen to drape
the delicate sheets of their art

                    ☧

each spider toils a tiny allotment
paving with crystalline filaments
a single square inch of air

spires spun of mist turrets of frost
this city will not stand
ten thousand years ten winters
ten weeks until summer fallow

each night that feudal lord
the wind like a second thought
rends the structure
confiscating rags to repair
the underbellies of cloud

✠

across this tattered white page
ten million spiders swarm
the living ink of their spinning
writing a letter to be read
when all moments coincide

meantime they mend the torn shroud
adorning the veil
with the gleaming black pearls
of their bodies

revealing the face of a bride
hiding who she will turn out to be

RING-NECKED PHEASANT

Thudding of hooves
in the damp leafy forest,
terrible squealing
of boars. Thrown from
her hunter, the king's
young wife breaks her neck
on the trunk of an oak.
Acorns fall like tears.

Years go by and without
his knowledge the king's
loneliness makes a pact
with ungovernable
things dwelling beneath
the soil. Loosestrife,
plentiful cities spring up
in the untilled fields.

Now the king eyes
the Milliners' Guild bill
with approval. His new
bride will be sporting
gold-dipped plumes
of four and twenty pheasant,
bare tables of the peasantry
plucked carcasses

for the feast. On the day,
a solemn chill
weather blows in
with the priests and during
the ceremony brushes
penance like crumbs
from the groom's tight
lips. The bride crushes

the posy of jonquils
in her fist. Her quill
caplet lifts like a wing
in the breeze, ghostly
gears flap its pinions.
Tears, a rain
of feathery clapping
as she receives the kiss.

WASP'S NEST

Autumn has gnawed the broad
hands from the maples, poplar leaves
darken like meat. The path unravelling
like a roll of gauze reveals it now
in the arbour's ribs, a scorched organ
dangling from green arterial stems.

All summer long the wasps
have mummified their fury,
bound themselves within
a mâché of spit and vegetable pages
torn unread from the trees. The old news
our lives are blindly shaped from
while we try to set happiness
asway. Weather-pulped,
wind-frayed, this charred grey piñata
that seems likely to crumble
like ash at the gentlest touch
is tough to break open

as the human heart. Lantern illuminating
nothing, its searing yellow light
extinguished with an early frost.
Somewhere inside, the wintering queen,
a slumbering ember, glows.

SOWS' EARS

Every part of the pig but the squeal.
   —Meat Packers' motto

Articulate as arrowheads, the ears
piled in a bulk-aisle bin like a mound
of dead leaves rustle imperceptibly
when touched. Slightly greasy, stiff
triangular scraps of improperly cured
vellum, amber leather that smells a bit
of old baseball mitt. Snouts and trotters
gone to market, artifacts of the body's
lost culture. To be the unlikely bearers
of story, to be the captured flags of
a glorious mud-and-gut empire, is to be
reduced to oversized tortilla chips
for cockapoos togged out in tartan
rain gear. Gristle marks the edge unhinged
from the hog's grinning head, each severed
flap of skin a trap door revealing that dark
bristly tunnel to the brain, a petrous trough
into which sound once poured like funnelled grain:
snuffle, squeal, snore, amorous grunt
of boar, voracious slurp of suckling pig,
the farmer at chow time yelling *soo-eeey!*
Here was hoarded cheerful oink
of sow in farrow.

         Now: silence. Unlike
delicate pink shells, when held to the ear
these transmit no porcine echo of the sea.
Nor like the runtiest toe in the litter
do they cry a solo rendition of
we we we when pinched between finger
and thumb. But they are not dumb. A symphony
is scored in the faded maroon ink
of shrivelled veins, its sorrowful un-
remembered strains stored in the stopped
blood of swine. Settling, the sallow heap
scrapes like an audience taking its chairs. Some
of the ears prick up to listen. Some hear.

✠

III

DEAR PETER

✠

And sure, if fate some future bard shall join
In sad similitude of griefs to mine,
Condemn'd whole years in absence to deplore,
And image charms he must behold no more;
Such if there be, who loves so long, so well;
Let him our sad, our tender story tell;
The well-sung woes will soothe my pensive ghost;
He best can paint 'em, who shall feel 'em most.

—Alexander Pope, "Eloisa to Abelard"

✠

RIDDLE FOR TWO VOICES STAGED IN A CONFESSION STALL

[B]y a kind of holy presage of his name he marked you out to be especially his when he named you Heloise, after his own name, Elohim.
—Abelard to Heloise, *Letter 4*

HELOISE

ABELARD

what melts in the mouth
like manna, is slippery as shrimp
nets woven of seaweed, echoes
on a chill slow breeze

beats me

the rose petal you lick
like a postage stamp when you send me
thoughts penned in transparent
pink veins

something to fondle
in your pocket
or dissect during moments of
boredom?

[wind chime]
a tame sun dog yawns

carved in a clamshell
you keep tight-lipped
as a locket

opening wide the Elohim gate
the blue maw wavers
[gong]

a broken stuttering
of spokes on the bicycle
you ride as you stroke yourself to sleep

flat tire
remember

(and after, does it stink
like roofing tar? is it sour
as twice-chewed gum?
do you scour it from your tongue
as a pigherd scrapes glaur from his boot?)

nope
nope
and nope,
it's heady as a hemp bush
burning in a dope bust
incinerator

HELOISE	ABELARD

the tenderest blasphemy
I ache to hear
you utter –

                                            just say it

my Name.

                    [awkward pause]

                                              so, what sounds like
                                              a heliotrope
                                              holding back a sneeze…

PREQUEL

*How great an interest the talent of your own
wisdom pays daily to the Lord in the many
spiritual daughters you have borne for him,
while I remain totally barren and labour in
vain amongst the sons of perdition!*
—Abelard to Heloise, *Letter 4*

In the movie version,
a handsome investigative priest
dispatched by the Vatican
gathers like windfall
evidence of your immaculate
ripening. The luscious nun
turns out to be a double
agent for the forces of Evil,
and several coincident deaths
involving out-of-control Mack trucks
are foreshadowed: fade in to
the holy font sizzling like a hot spring.

An awkward flash-forward
reveals how Satan's minions
will steal from drunk-on-duty seraphim
the cryogenic spunk stored
in lambskin safes. The fertility clinic
explosion blows the budget
for special effects, but the caterer
is a dab hand with ketchup
and, with an umbilicus
fashioned from blanched asparagus,
the guy playing you
throttles himself convincingly enough.

In real life you perform
your own stunts. When you descend
the cellar stairs those ominous
grunts are the infant stirrings
of a half-nursed longing
interred in the ossuary
beneath your heart's dirt floor.
I can smell it on your breath,
the tangy ferment
of ensilaged apples. A greasy halo
hovers around your robed torso
like a mirage quivering on asphalt.

That expectant glow
is just sweat condensing
on the outside of the glass. What matters
is the liquid it contains:
like tiny green spiders, a million
emotions swarm
inside you. With the infinite
patience of one who loves
his vocation, he who handles the obstinate
calvings readies his chains
to pull, head or hoof first,
a pliable creature from the ruminant soul.

This isn't about
the fifty-cent pool with bets
on birth weight and
Good versus Evil. The subtext is
simply my fear. I watch
the papyrus credits unscroll
while a horror-show soundtrack plinks
in my ear, a clunky, tuneless lullaby
plunked out on silver spoons. With
tarnished caws a crow heralds
The End, the terrifying
untossed coin of your coming.

FRAGMENT 19

]
      ] then I knew your heart
]
            ] *ketchup*
            thick rubbery
            blob like
            dried paint [
]
]
a partly opened can of corned beef,
the aluminum strip [
]
                        ] broken
]
            ] *a thinner*
            smear
            like a bloody
            fingerprint [
]
the key [

SINGALONG *SOUND OF MUSIC*

*You know too how when you were pregnant and I
took you to my own country you disguised yourself
in the sacred habit of a nun, a pretence which was an
irreverent mockery of the religion you now profess.*
—Abelard to Heloise, *Letter 4*

I told Uncle you were taking me
to the movies and here we are
following the family Von Trapp
to safety beyond the Alps.

                  In the queue:
a man of cheerless demeanour
wearing an egg-yellow sweater
and a name tag reading *Ray,
a Drop of Golden Sun*; his companion,
Men on the Road with a Load to Tote,
drags behind her on a rope
a box the size of an infant's coffin.
I swear something moved inside
but at the wicket I forgot it
when the manager refused
to honour my vow of poverty
by issuing free tickets.

My scalp itches beneath this veil
stapled to a makeshift wimple
cut from a white plastic jug.
Brother Hugo's old habit
bears metal-scented traces
of the bitter Job-like rages
his lobotomy failed to cure. A sure
sign of stress or imbalance,

my left sleeve is inches longer
than the right. You, on the other hand,
squirm in Nazi britches a size too small
and struggle to hit a low note
during "I Am Sixteen Going on Seventeen"
when *Dough a Dear* squeezes by your knees
in a scanty suit stitched from Monopoly
money. Like the restorative effect
of tap water on Sea-Monkeys,
the smell of buttered popcorn revivifies
resentments pent up in my chest.

A liquorice-cud-chewing choir, the audience
rises in unison from red velvet pews,
lighters aloft and swaying like tapers. Singing
"Edelweiss" soothes the savage heart
beating within the collective breast.
Dressed as a sheep a small boy bleats
"Bless my old man forever."

Skipping the homeland isn't as simple
as slipping through the schoolyard's
chain-link fence at recess
used to be. We return to the car to find
someone has removed the distributor cap.
Spent as a lover, it lies in an oily puddle,
embraced by its own four arms. You take
my last quarter to phone the tow truck
and when I slip my hand back into my cassock

pennies drop behind the false pocket
and fall on the pavement
like manna. By accident
I've discovered the secret opening
to the rose bush of the soul, the hidden
slit one enters to scratch
the thorniest itch. The thought
of St. Benedict's holy underwear
blooms on a branch like a national flower,
a tattered grey warning marking the border
between what is and what will be.

Beneath the robe cool night air
reaches up and strokes my bare skin.
Your boots pacing the parking lot
smack of the Baroness slapping
that riding crop against her palm. Under
pale street light the straight pins
glinting on my tucked-up sleeve
are the center line on a dark highway:
road going nowhere, glittering spine
of a serpent chasing its own tail.

DUSK

If since our conversion from the world to God I have not yet written you any word of comfort or advice, it must not be attributed to indifference on my part but to your own good sense, in which I have always had such confidence that I did not think anything was needed...
—Abelard to Heloise, *Letter 2*

Puffballs dry as stale
bread crumbs lead along the road's
weedy spine. Beneath my boot heel
I burst them in a series
of blood-brown explosions.

The reservoir, a big square basin
deep enough to wash the Lord's weary feet,
sits cooling in the field, heat
rises from the water's dusty skin.
The faded signs posted on the fence
read *Danger: Thin Ice.* All summer long
I've been following your trail of evasions
like some scavenger of discarded butts,
gleaning whatever unfiltered
tip of suggestion has been
touched by your lips
then stubbed out. Skating a line
between paranoia
and insight. I really don't want
to break through.

A few elusive fireflies
flit above the marsh. They hover
with post-coital languor, lit
cigarettes of invisible lovers lying
hidden by grasses in the lengthening dark.
With a sniper's ruthless aim
I sight them
between forefinger and thumb
and snuff them out.
They spark and flicker
back to life like a distant
scattering of lamps, a forbidden
city that extinguishes itself
the instant I set out toward its light.

FRAGMENT 52

]
]
         ] and potatoes! [

   ] thoughts [
]
]
buried under the ground
]

SAME STORY, DIFFERENT DAY

[Y]ou know what my uncontrollable desire did with
you there, actually in a corner of the refectory, since
we had nowhere else to go.
—Abelard to Heloise, *Letter 4*

On visiting day
the prisoners sit at long tables
with their backs against the wall
like a row of orange traffic cones
waiting to be knocked over,
or a strange assortment of fruit
washed up together on a bleak
cinder-block shore:
Blood Oranges, bitter
Sevilles, Navels with thick
pitted rinds, unripened
little Mandarins. An assembly
of cenobites robed in the tangerine
garb of the grease monkey.
My man's coverall
is too big for him, ill-
fitting prison-issue skin
I can't unpeel.

The night before sentencing
we made love so many times
we were sore, storing it up
for the dry stretch ahead. Already
we have nothing
much to say. I ask when
I should bring his clothes,
does he need the zippered boots
I secretly want to throw out
because they make his feet stink.

On my left a woman reads aloud
the fortune in her husband's hand.
Beside us a man goes fishing
with his tongue for the prize
in his girlfriend's mouth.

One of the guards
is checking me out so I try
to look pretty while manning
the kissing booth. Across
the bare plywood table, my guy
holds my wrists and sneaks
the balloon full of contraband dreams
I smuggled in up my sleeve. My heart,
though I've emptied its chambers,
set off the metal detector
and is being held in a locker
with my pocket change and purse.

☩

Here, the Abbot guards
his dark flock. While the inmates dine
he watches the refectory
like a warden. I'll never learn
to talk intimately

across this cafeteria table. We fuck
each other quickly
with our eyes. Observing us
from the garden window,
a cement statue of Our Lady
in menopause blushes
green beneath her lichen beard,
pretends to check a chipped fingernail.

I ask if you want salt. I don't know
what else to say. Beside us an angel
arm-wrestles Brother John
who is trying to win himself
a stuffed pink heart. The oblate
to my right examines her soul
in that funhouse mirror,
the back of her spoon.

Amid this black carnival
where you have pitched
your hand-hemmed 50/50 tent
against the world, I bathe
in the rainstorm of your gaze.
Camels fill their humps
with tears, with sighs women come
to gather stolen glimpses
in heavy jugs. I pour your swift
grey glances into my jar. I drink
you in, store you up.

OLIVE BRANCH

How unseemly for those holy hands which now turn
the pages of sacred books to have to perform degrading
services in women's concerns!
—Abelard to Heloise, *Letter 4*

I arouse myself from sleep with my own mouth
on my palm, tenderly kissing the thick pouch of flesh
beneath the thumb, purse teeming with stars,
the irredeemable currency I would spend to have you
in my hands, in my mouth, my body, my bed.
I would cut out this tongue that will never taste yours,
tear the thumbs from these dumb flightless birds
that will never flutter like doves seeking land
to roost on your warm limbs.

Yet a thousand miles distant I can feel you
move in me with the slow liquid heat of a desire
that could seed clouds, cleanse the pale moon,
flood its vanished waterways with longing.
I smell your tears on my face, hear your need moaned
low into my ear, and softly, from the hidden chamber,
a frail hopeful choir, castrati of the heart, once more
begins to sing.

FRAGMENT 73

]
]
pouring hard [
]
        ] and tears [
]
silverfish streaming from the mouldering stacks

                ] important pages
]
]
devoured and destroyed [
     ] my antiquarian [

            ] heart.

YES AND NO

Heloise my sister, once dear to me in
the world, now dearest to me in Christ,
logic has made me hated by the world.
—*Abelard's Confession of Faith*

Devoted heretic, rewarded
for your efforts
with an eviction notice,
your philosophy was simple –
find a place where
the thorniest contradictions
could peaceably coexist.
The last time I saw you
you were moving
from a grey area of faith
to an open concept space
constructed solely of questions:

 Would the animal shelter
 find a home for your
 ancient one-eyed tabby?

 Did God the Father,
 like a heavenly sea horse cradling comets
 in the pipe bowl of his belly,
 or a holy penguin in an arctic
 of unending patience coddling the egg
 of Christ's being on chilblained feet,
 actually birth his own son?

 Do you still love me (assuming
 you once did)?

 Yes
and no, black and white, hot
and cold. A stew of antonyms
sustained you like a hobo's dish
of sautéed boot. As proof
we were poles apart

you opened your fridge to reveal
the package of snow peas
you intended to subsist upon
for the balance of your tenancy
on Earth. The cardboard boxes
I'd brought from the liquor store
were heavier empty than you
might imagine. Even now, it doesn't bear
thinking, you on your knees
after midnight in the circum-
fused light of one unpacked lamp,
trying in vain to fit everything in.
As if an earthquake had shaken
open all the cupboards in your head,
the floor was strewn with pill
bottles, undeveloped negatives,
pages of sheet music out of
Guitar Hits from the Sixties
and the same leaky wineskin
we used on our honeymoon.

In the midst of such ruin
the smell of Earl Grey tea brewing
over the steady flame of books
crackling in the wood stove
was a welcome comfort.
Like the leaves
of the coffee plant you grew
from a bean into a gangly stalk
I once deemed aesthetically
annoying, our old familiarities
had withered from lack
of attention. How strange it felt
to be drinking once more
from the last of those unbreakable
white mugs rimmed
around the lip with blue
flowers! Cheery, testy,

and reserved by turns, we coughed
politely into our cuffs, ignoring
the embarrassment of smoke
in an atmosphere grown mildly
poisonous. Your magnanimity
regarding my impending nuptials
irked me. Reduced to living
on tips saved up in a pickle jar,
you gave me a piece
of unleavened advice
with which I was to buy
a loaf of whole grain bread
on my way back to the nunnery.

You swore I would taste
the difference between us
like day and night. Weary of pondering
the long and short of it all
– buy high, sell low?–
by the time I left
my pockets were weighted
with wooden nickels.
When you waved at the door
I could see from the Taser
scorch on your palm
how you'd been pinned
like a butterfly against
a brisk and cloudless sky, hung
out to dry, rumpled shirt
washed once too often. Old love,
dear heart, now that you've slipped
the stigmata of clothes pegs,
escaped my unforgiving grip
to fall crumpled as a leaf
into a final pile of ironing,
allow me to admit how deeply
I regret not kissing you
hello and goodbye.

FRAGMENT 91

```
                 ] forget
cleanly          ]
torn             ] your heart's
in two           ] forever.
left side        ] ticking as if
destroyed        ]
                 ] taking you home.
                 ]
                 ] an engine
                 ] One day
                 ] turn
                 ]
                 ] over. Trust me.
                 ] Nothing
                 ]
                 ] forever, even grief
                 ]
                 ] dependable!
                 ] rusts
                 ]
```

ASTROLABE

*And so we were caught in the act as the poet says
happened to Mars and Venus. Soon afterwards the
girl found that she was pregnant, and immediately
wrote me a letter full of rejoicing to ask what I
thought she should do. One night then, when her
uncle was away from home, I removed her secretly
from his house, as we had planned, and sent her
straight to my own country. There she stayed with
my sister until she gave birth to a boy, whom she
called Astralabe.*
—Abelard, *The Story of His Misfortunes*

The solar system dangles
on fine-gauge fishing line. I
may be out of my element,
Teacher Dear, but I often lie
down here to seek meaning
on the indigo ceiling
stippled with glow-in-the-dark stars.
My research reveals that
Saturn is composed of Styrofoam
and haloed with a stainless steel
oven ring. Along with an eel
and a bleach bottle, Neptune
was discovered in Uncle's herring net
the morning after
a mysterious eclipse: note
how the Blue Planet is the same
glassy hue as the Sea King's cold
scrotum. Pluto, a Ping-Pong
ball, bounces along the galactic plane
conducting a melody light years old,
invisible to the naked eye.

Sentimental music makes
my nipples itch. Despite
determined twiddling of the dial
I still pull in the same curdled signal,
shaggy as the ecstatic
tussle of interplanetary dust
bunnies breeding beneath the bed.
With the clarity peculiar
to us oxygen tipplers I recall
the infamous homemade astrolabe
at our son's grade eight science fair –
two cardboard circles pinned together
with a grommet, sights drawn
with banana-scented marker –
the ensuing kafuffle
when he taught the other children
how to calculate the angles
of Venus and Mars tumbling
in their star-besmirched
quilts. Eventually, a boy
will outgrow outer space.

Rocket men in souped-up
aluminum squid
trail flatulent lilac emissions
across the wallpaper. Indelible as a cloud
of cuttlefish ink, the nocturnal
perfume of an unscrubbed teenage neck
malingers in the pillow,
and little toy figures stand
posed in permanent combat,
a space crew abandoned
like outgrown drinking buddies
dressed in the futuristic

jerkins of yore (which reminds me
of you and that ponytail
braided from pantyhose
you'd attach to your hair
like a clip-on tie or a donkey tail
whenever you saw the old gang,
how it hung down your back
like a surrogate spine – I knew
you were never suited
to the station wagon).

You'll be happy to hear
I've adopted a baby doll
with one hinged blue eye
stuck halfway shut
and a working cloaca I use
to water the narcissus in the window.
She has the choir-conducting
pinkies of a born tea drinker,
each tiny knuckle dimpled
with plastic fat. A ticklish
fancy now feathers my vacant nest,
and I sleep with a slender
telescoped yearning which has lost
its focus but, on rare nights,
when the air is musky with moonbeam,
extends itself to sniff out the familiar
route around the Milky Way.
I still throw my share of bones
to the Dog Star, that sly beggar.
With practice, I'm attuning
my ear to the distant celestial
tinkling of the spheres.

DETAIL FROM AN ILLUMINATION

*Moreover, fashion itself is the badge of the pimp
and betrays his lewd mind, as it is written: 'A
man's clothes and the way he laughs and his gait
betray his character.'*
—Abelard to Heloise, *Letter 7*

The artist has a wicked sense
of humour. You should sue him
for that hat, tasselled like a boy
baby's plump genitalia, gangrenous grey
casserole lid beneath which you stew,
sporting a wary pout. I wear
the merest smirk, my chin bandaged
in a wimple. With a few simple
strokes he has outlined my veil
in white against my habit,
the way chalk marks
the shape of a body on blacktop.

How young we look, casualties
of fashion, our outfits hopelessly
outdated in front of those hideous
curtains. Under that hempen robe
you're wearing your favourite
red long johns and poking
the toe of one slim tapered boot
beneath my skirt. The other leg
is hooked over your knee
like a carefully latched gate.

What tortured thoughts
were you hiding
beneath that bloody cap?
A brain-hued blue, all those ideas
plopped upon your fringed orange locks
like organ meat. My own cranium
appears oddly swollen, as if
my headdress housed a beehive
of backcombed syllogisms. We
seem to be speaking in
some sort of sign language.

Either you are making a point
or complaining
there's a button missing from your cuff.

I'm playing you a tune
on an invisible squeezebox, showing you
how big it was,
the one that got away.

FRAGMENT 147

]
       ] sobs [
]
Soft [
]
]
]
      ] useless [
]
pelts of small animals.

ANOTHER DAY IN THE SCRIPTORIUM

*Jerome, the greatest doctor of the Church and glory of
the monastic profession, in exhorting us to love of letters,
says: 'Love knowledge of letters and you will not love the
vices of the flesh'...*
—Abelard to Heloise, *Letter 7*

Downpour. Dreams dissolving
in a denture mug. Snug oblivion
breached by the carillon alarm,
a cruel harpoon of light drags me
from the shallow refuge sought
in my cups each soul-dark night. Sloshed
ablutions with tallow in a basin,
a ladle of gruel, then the lint brush,
brisk flagellum. Fuelled
by duty and destroyed ambition, I board
the rush hour train with herds
of drugged pilgrims shrugging off
sloth, and drag my sorry cross
through the stations of my day.

I greet my sister scriveners
as we remove dripping cloaks,
complaining of our ills and the weather.
The stockroom stinks like wet dog,
damp vellum. Each morning as I scour
with a lunellum the skin
stretched on the frame, I remember
shaving your unlimed, living cheek. Earwax
and urine added to lampblack, I mix
a batch of ink. We pour ourselves
into our work, feather quills
scraping the page, sallow under
fluorescents flickering down rain-dimmed
halls, eyes on the water clock.

At coffee break I calculate
my reward upon release from this vale
of steer's hide and squib: salary (naught,
that rash vow of poverty) ×
years served (seems like Eternity) ×
a percentage of your puny
interest in me = payback –
a pension in Paris, double berth
in a five-star cemetery, resting place
for our portable bones. At last,
a marble lid on our troubles. Beneath
prim stone poses, on a mattress of roses,
we'll sail toward a recessionary sun
and, storied, sink into the earth's

perennial plot. Meanwhile, my cubicle
confines me as the borders
of the page imprison this book, and in
space the size of a Suffolk ewe
I overwrite old laws with new
on parchment scrubbed clean
with bran and raw milk. Pee break,
I look in the mirror and think
I could have been a poet living
on windfalls; a prostitute the avails;
a realtor the subprime greed
of speculators. The oath I swore
(*airtight as this hermetically sealed
office, unbreachable as your cast-iron
honour*) has penned me here, but
I've come to love my cell

the way a horse jogging back
to the paddock at darkfall answers
the call of the nosebag. Staff room:
a market stall, source of lip balm, spices
and sex toys. Bryce: the blue-eyed
eunuch from the male room
delivering our daily envelopes,

fingertips arousing my palm.
Dress code: drab, careerists all
in black. Those guilt-flavoured
Name Day cakes baked of quinoa
by bossy Euphemia and the pent-up
estrogen of sister brides – enough
drama to spark sororicide!

Of an evening I set out tins
for tea and watch a movie
from the safety of a foldaway
settee. "Doctor, a nun is not a person
who wishes or desires." At the end
Audrey Hepburn rings a bell
and a bitter portress hands her
sackcloth for the sacked,
regalia of the damned. Changed,
she stands on the threshold of
a blinding, fearful freedom. Hell,
that searcher might be me.
When I eloped I lost
my underscript, a palimpsest

rolled up in an unread hide
mapping the untapped
acorn of my soul that lies
on a frigid Tibetan slope,
buried there by a prudent squirrel.
Like a page left on the copier,
an unsent fax, I surrender
My Love to Your Will,
this sanctioned erasure. O! but
my dreams – those vines bearing
strange, luscious fruit, lutes
vibrating with silvery music and
bright feathered creatures
peering from the fronds:

my randy monks, my ape-faced
drolleries, my errant, wanton truant's marginalia!

EPITAPH FOR THE LAST OF THE RED HOT LOVERS

[Y]ou granted a rare privilege in token of your love and sincerity: a trental
of masses to be said on my behalf by the abbey of Cluny after my death.
—Heloise to the Abbot of Cluny, *Letter 167*

Here lies a matchless passion igniter
extinct as a spark without a lighter.
From lack of love the Lusty One
succumbed to spontaneous combustion.

＋

IV

THE LOST LETTERS

＋

u cn gt a gd jb w hi pa!
So thinks a sign in the subway.
Think twice when letters disappear
Into Commodity's black hole –
No turning back from that career.
This counter-spell may save your soul.
—James Merrill, "If U Cn Rd Ths"

＋

IVORY

Wistful and giddy as a snuffbox
lacking its lid. Illicit as a spinster's
string of contraband beads. Fecund
as a fertility goddess
chiselled twenty thousand years ago
from a mammoth tooth.

Look, darling – there,
amid the other loves
time has whittled into trinkets,
heaped among harvested tusks
like a pair of sickle moons
hacked glorious and gleaming
from a midnight sky,
where poachers smugly
pose on ivory hammocks,
stacked in the stockpile
of raw story: that's us!

Like the keys on a piano
whose strings have rusted
into fence wire corralling
muffled herds of sound,
we make beautiful music together.
We're lucky as weighted dice,
fated forever to roll
sham wins. In our final
befuddled moment
we are doomed as the white king
about to be mated. Hopelessly,
bravely, blindly devoted
as a pipe stem pulling
the last wisp of opium
to the brink
of an endangered dream.

ROTARY DIAL TELEPHONE

Your black handset droops in the cradle
like the floppy uncropped ears
of the neighbour's Doberman, unnaturally silent
since his vocal chords were cut. He too
once roamed long distances, sniffing out bitches,
pissing his number on poles
while the lines above tossed out
an assortment of late night longings
like sticks. Double cheese pizza.
Something – anything – to fill the gap,
the awkward pause, the painful revealing
silence on the other end. Junior calling
for bail same month the taxes came due.

Loyal outmoded friend, mute witness
to cruel laughter, gentle lies, the most terrible tidings
of loss, your Master's Voice is forever guarded
in that square, unremembering head. These days
his finger determinedly dragging your collar
around and back and around and back
commands much simpler business.

✠

In the calcification of an afternoon snooze
arthritic Blacky farts and frets
about the cat's essential nature, unable to decide
whether its green or amber eye
is the soul's true barometer. After dialling
the podiatrist to book a Tuesday appointment,
Mrs. Pritchett clacks a spoon against a can
yelling *din din!* Next door a feeble half-ring
jingles the stillness, but it's just the telephone
chasing off wrong numbers in its sleep. No one
but that pesky market surveyor who persists
in asking which brand of mint best sweetens
the breath ever calls.

COMPANY TOWN

In the softwood-scented bar
of the last hotel
open for business, no one talks
layoffs anymore but severance
packages, retraining, NHL –
peanut-eating asylum seekers chalking up
pool cues and losses, their cable cut off,
wives sent to cities to find work
as Walmart greeters and scout
pet-friendly basement suites.
They watch their team tank
in the playoffs. A stripper grinds
the pole deeper into unplanned
obsolescence, her mechanistic
scissor kicks barely raising
a sweat on their beer glasses
and failing to jump-start
the local economy.

            On life support
the paper mill emits hisses
of steam and eggy belches
of undigested wood. Engine
from another age, dormant beast
on a dead planet, it is housed
in an unheated pavilion of pipes
dripping with its condensing breaths,
and tended by two cenobitic supers
who administer oils and press
ominous black buttons, sacrificing sleep
in alternating shifts to keep
its juices flowing. Each fiscal-tide
they set the silenced rods a-pump
and sluice the stagnant vats,
in case they one day need
to prod the thing, get it up
and running.

            Outside, in the tracks
of her growling blue shadow
a cougar glides down
from the clearcuts to snack
on abandoned cats. Burghers
of the sub-boreal, bands
of bleak-eyed raccoons
foreclose on garbage cans,
redundant prowlers wringing
gloved hands, lamenting
the glory years of bins
rich with plate scrapings. Wishbone
and gristly rib, ossified runes
inscribed with well-loved recipes
for Boulevard and Terrace.
A just-add-water instant
town, all its best-laid plans
upended.

          For Sale signs
fallen on lawns gone to thistle.
Windows unwashed as houses
go blind beneath tarps
tacked over leaks – inside,
squirrels redecorate. Wasps
hang paper lanterns in the eaves.
Like leaves on unwatered dahlias,
Pee Wee pennants droop in empty
arenas, ice rink and swimming pool
echoing desuetude. *Shush*-ing by habit
the silence, the school librarian
airs the unread
books. Shelves half-empty
at the 24-7, and the mini-mall
sign missing letters – commerce
unkempt as the mouth of a man
with no dental plan.

               A family
of beavers whets their teeth
felling timber, not afraid to get
their feet wet. All business, oily
brush cuts, Castor and Sons.
New construction, a cul-de-sac
bending the river. Architects
of Optimism, *If we build it,*
they will come. Amped as an elk
in rut, with tense snorts
of exhaust a muscle car circles
the park, past a drunk
debating the downturn
with a hydrant. A masked
graffitist tags a totem,
intent on destruction. Woodpeckers
write resumés on the unbleached
bark of trees.

BLUE PUMPS

The new pumps worn by the man who waves at strangers
are in the style favoured by England's Queen Mother:
royal blue and stout
                              of heel.

☩

Wearing patched cast-off pants cinched with a safety pin,
a dead twig accessorizing this season's soiled acrilon sweater,

he models his new shoes
down the sidewalk,
cement runway.

Blue pumps provide an elegant foundation.

In fashion one starts at the bottom and works up.

☩

While sturdy,
blue pumps are not earthquake proof.

☩

The world is armed with a billion
pairs of identical
blue pumps, battalions of blue
pumps marching from assembly lines
in China.

They come in different sizes,
of course, and some of those
who buy them have two
                    left feet
while others lack
                    one leg.

☩

Two square barges pass in the channel.

The blue pumps ferry their wearer across a long
puddle.

☩

The crazy directs communications
between the sky and his blue pumps.

If red shoes make you dance, do blue shoes
make you fly?

☩

Innocents, brand new,
their shiny leather
skins unscuffed.

Not suede, but blue, so
                    don't step on them.

CHARITY

Hunched, hands in jean pockets, he crossed the sill
and asked if coats were free, for it was cold
and he'd no money. From my station at the till
I offered him his pick from the dollar rack.
I knew him instantly – prematurely old
with dirt and drink, the toil of scavenging bins
for bottles – and waited while he thumbed
through stacks of used clothes for him to see me
as I saw him: a child. Of scant promise, frog-eyed,
slow, twin stunted by a runt-eating brother,
bullied by boys, by girls taunted at recess.

In our grade six pageant I'd played mother
to his pauper (stiffly, and chagrined
that though he struggled to learn his part,
he was better than me), the teacher's pet
project who conquered the gym, earning the hearts
of classmates and parents, all of us
oxen yoked to the ploughboy's performance.
Propped up in the dirndl I'd steeped in a vat
of dye as if it were a potion for courage,
and a peasant blouse, the costume that won
my audition, I toed my mark and muttered
each line with a gulp, marvelling as "My son!"
strode fearlessly the fiefdoms of the stage,
seeking his fortune. When the princess,
a full foot taller, bent to kiss her swain,
he doffed his tinfoil crown and croaked
out a punchline that brought down the house.

Now, stepped from decades of gleaning gutters,
he'd returned to what was possible, a man
grown into his fate like a foot into a boot.

Who knows what losses he had suffered,
what oceans crossed, mountains climbed to arrive
at such a state (I've seen him since, half-soaked
in mythos, boarding the morning bus
in bleak confusion, once pushing a cart
under the drawbridge where ragged souls,
guardians of the moat, huddle at the footings).
Yet that day he wasn't seeking pity.
From beyond the backdrops of our city
he'd returned – still short, *spunky* – to visit
his mom, he said, and hadn't brought a coat.

I saw my own life had been driven
by small-heeled struggle, the leather scuffed
but snug, and that for a long while I'd been
walking the wrong way in a costume slowly
going out of style. I tightened the strings
of my shopkeeper's apron, awaiting
some mention of my forgettable role.
If he remembered, he acted as though
we'd never met. I sensed him sparing me
a show, should it shame us to recall the stars
extinguished in the children we once were:
the miscast crone stirring her empty pot,
the halfwit hero who sets out penniless
and returns with a title and an ermine stole.

No curtain call. He'd come only to claim
a cloak against the weather. Nothing fit.
"Try Saint Vinnie's," I said. The sky looked like snow.
And wished him luck, but didn't speak his name.

THE TEXADA QUEEN

We had words, I recall: too much beer
in me at seventeen, sarcasm thrust like a sword
I couldn't parry. It was Christmas, or New Year's;

I cracked my glass on my father's brow,
(as my mother in a pillbox hat once broke
a bottle of champagne across the prow

of a ferry he designed – launching thus
their lives in the new country). No one moved. No one spoke
as the blood, unstaunched, began to trickle

from the gash. *Like Zeus, unzipped,*
the third eye weeping, I later thought – much
later. Then my youngest brother tipped

the ashtray as he tried to pluck bits
of glass from the beer-drenched rug
now awash in fear and cigarettes,

and my father slipped his moorings, shrugged off
my mother's arm and shot between the chairs
to chase me through the basement, tugging

at my shirt. I outstripped him on the stairs,
then tripped over the threshold. In he lurched,
and briskly boxed my ears. Within my tangled hair,

a swatted bug, I hid out on the porch
a while until my skull ceased buzzing,
the lamp jar above me full of scorched flies.

Now I remember my ears ringing
as my father's must have rung all those years
of tending boilers in freighters bringing

spoils across the ocean. His hearing gone,
he's telling me a story, but the words
fall overboard like drowning men, their names

sunk to the bottom (this is one I've heard,
off San Francisco the ship tossed by storms
so rough the captain bid his crew goodbye

and, braving the gale alone to save them,
went on deck to dump the timber load,
his life no longer a sure thing). Decades on,

I try to salvage the scattered lumber
of our conversation, yelling to be heard
across a café table, over our tumblers

of milk, as my father grapples for words.
"That place you lose your money, what's it called?"
"Casino," I shout. "Persuade?" "Cholesterol!"

"It's a bastard," he says. His brain is over-full,
crowded with a cargo of memories
now waking, banging about inside the hull

like famine victims after a long crossing.
Hauled up into sunlight's glare, they blink –
nit-ridden, dragging goats his father ferried

across the Clyde and a brother stinking
of the diphtheria ward, a cousin shorn
after scarlet fever – then stare blankly

at the world. The stuff of lockets, foreign
to me. I can't help my father recover
their names, the lost blueprint for morning,

or the boat they sailed in on. Powerless,
we leave them at the dock, links of blood
pudding in their pockets. And then the hour

of my birth arrives in a vivid flood –
"Like a wee skinned rabbit you were," he beams –
and brings me up squalling, covered in blood.

THE JAR

When the first frost grew
like hair on dead grass and the idea
of snow was new, she swaddled
banknotes in wax paper,
and sealed the bundle, unlikely fruit,
in a canning jar, the maker's name
raised like a welt on the glass.
Beneath an aspen by the creek
he dug a hole, his shovel
ringing on the rocky soil.
She wrapped the jar in a towel
and set it in the ground; he filled
the vault with dirt then marked
the axis of their fortune
with a stone. They buried it
as a dog buries a bone,
to be dug up later
when taxes came due in spring.

All winter their cattle trod
a frozen trail beside the creek, dried
to a trickle, to drink water
she drew from the well and poured
into a clawfoot tub in the yard,
cast-iron relic from a Gold Rush
boudoir. After her husband drove off
to the mill each morning
she propped the baby in the wagon
with blankets so he wouldn't fall out,
then dropped the dip-pail on a rope,
drew it up full, and cracked the ice
in the tub, the bottom of the bucket

clanging. Coin-coloured, copper
and gold heifers stood watching
like goddesses waiting for their bath
to be drawn, steam from their nostrils
freezing on feathery white lashes
as back and forth she trudged
between well and tub while the baby fussed.
She poured, and poured, a slave
to their thirst. Then went inside
to boil water on the wood stove
and bathe first her son
then herself, in the sink.

Weary from toil, at night the two
played crib by lamplight, drinking
jug wine, stoking the fire before
sleep, trying to keep the house
warm. Winter seemed never-ending. Because
they were young they bickered
sometimes about money out of
boredom, and sometimes turned on
the transistor and danced cheek to cheek
in the wavering flame of a candle stub.

The inevitable envelope
arrived in the weekly mail
before the thaw. They waited until
ice melted and topsoil slid
like flesh down the mountain's
tired face. He got the shovel from the shed
and started to dig. He dug and dug,
down to gnarled roots that clutched
and grabbed for purchase
in the earth. The jar had disappeared

with the snow, displaced by the cattle's churning
hooves and meltwater pushing sludge
down the creek. Each began to doubt
the memory of the other – to which tree
had they entrusted their chattels, under
what hummock banked their hope?

While he worked sawing wood,
she dug. Now it was her job to retrieve
what had been lost, to believe
it was still there. Holes appeared
like signs in the hayfield where gophers
tunnelled in sympathy, and moles, fellow
minions of the dirt, lifted blind faces
to the sun and raised their pitchfork
paws in solidarity. Emissaries
from underground – if only
they could speak! Back humped
with determination, she dug until
her palms blistered, opening
every tree at the root. The shovel
thudded dully, disgorging
nothing but mud. *Where
ARE you?* she called out in despair. But
the wide-mouth jar was silent,
swallowed whole by the hill
which held dominion over them all.

Tax day came and went. Somehow –
a steer sold, overtime at the mill –
the bill was paid. But the jar within
the earth had drifted out of range
on currents of mud, shifted
the way buried bones get lost,
like dreams, settling into ruts.

Several summers on, the baby,
now a boy, was catching frogs
by the creek and found the jar
not far from where they'd planted it,
risen from the muck like a late blooming
bulb. His parents shook their heads
in wonder as he unscrewed
the rusted lid. The notes were damp
and outdated, the colour of play
money. How important that cache
had been made a funny story
now. Oddly saddened
that such luck had come
too late to matter much, she aired
the bills on the kitchen sill
and rinsed a whiff of mildew
from the jar that once preserved
notions by which they measured
their lives. She traced the script
upon the slippery soaped glass,
a message sent by younger selves
she no longer knew
how to read.

✝

NOTES

Dear Peter is inspired by the tragic love story of the brilliant student Heloise and her teacher, twelfth-century logician Peter Abelard. By most accounts, Abelard seduced the teenaged Heloise, and after the birth of their son and a secret marriage, Heloise's uncle Fulbert punished Abelard by having him castrated. Abelard continued his academic pursuits while Heloise reluctantly joined a convent.

Abelard's approach to religion, prescribing that faith must be subject to reason, met with resistance from established clerics who mistook his views for heresy. His talent for logic was paired with a lack of diplomacy, and his fraught career, punctuated by power struggles, saw him bounced around from abbey to abbey, suffering at times from poor health. Heloise, reluctant though she'd been to take the veil, and despite a lingering bitterness at being separated from her lover, seemed to possess innate managerial skills and became a well-regarded abbess. Eventually she read Abelard's publicly circulated account of his misfortunes, the *Historia Calamitatum,* and their famous correspondence began.

It's not known for certain if they ever saw each other again, but they were reunited in death when Heloise, who outlived Abelard by two decades, finally shared his grave. Over the following centuries their bones were disinterred and moved several times, finding a final destination in 1817 beneath their own carved effigies in a gothic tomb in France's Père Lachaise cemetery.

The poem "Yes and No" takes its title from one of Abelard's books, *Sic et Non*. The excerpts of letters used as epigraphs are taken from Penguin's *The Letters of Abelard and Heloise,* translated by Betty Radice. Other useful resources include *Heloise and Abelard: A New Biography,* by James Burge, and *The Lost Love Letters of Heloise and Abelard: Perceptions of Dialogue in Twelfth-Century France*, by Constant J. Mews.

✠

ACKNOWLEDGEMENTS

I'm grateful to many who have contributed to the existence of these poems. Thanks are due to the monks of St. Peter's Abbey in Saskatchewan for hospitality and inspiration, to Robert Kroetsch for suggesting Heloise and Abelard as a subject, and to the Chicks – Sugarlips, Dollface, Legs, and Pinstripe – for egging me on way back when, giving me my gangster name, and sticking together in Holy Chickdom. To the Canada Council for the Arts and the BC Arts Council for buying me some time, the Nice Ladies of SAFA at UVic for letting me take it, and the Schroeder-Browns for giving me some space. Other understanding supervisors, teachers, cat-sitters, and encouragers over the years, including Ross Leckie, Rebecca Fredrickson, the Sinclairs, and my family. The hard-working Brick team of Alayna, Cheryl, and Kitty, and my editor Stan Dragland, for his infallible honky ear and patience with these poems. Most of all, Steve Noyes, for morning coffee and real-life love poems.

Thanks also to the editors of the following publications, where earlier versions of some of these poems appeared: *Bei Mei Feng (North American Maple: A Literary Journal)*, *Border Crossings'* Special Venice Issue, *CV2*, *The Fiddlehead's* 1998 and 2006 Poetry Issues and The Essential West Coast Poetry & Fiction Issue, *Green Stone Mountain Review*, *The Malahat Review*, *The New Quarterly's* "Bad Men Who Love Jesus" Issue, *Pagitica in Toronto*, *Prairie Fire*, *Wascana Review*, *Listening with the Ear of the Heart: Writers at St. Peter's* (St. Peter's Press, 2003), *Long Journey: Contemporary Northwest Poets* (Oregon State University Press, 2006), and *Rock Salt: An Anthology of Contemporary BC Poetry* (Mother Tongue Publishing, 2008).

"Two Blue Elephants" was a runner up in *Pagitica in Toronto's* 2004 poetry contest. "Astrolabe" won the 2003 Banff Centre Bliss Carmen Award and received the Gold Award for poetry in the 2004 National Magazine Awards. Selections from these poems were shortlisted for the CBC Literary Awards in 2005 and 2006 under the titles *Ivory* and *Cell by Cell.* "The Texada Queen" was a finalist for the 2012 CBC Literary Prize and was published on the CBC Canada Writes website. "Lizard" was published on the Capital Verse website of the Greater Victoria Public Library. "Company Town," "Charity," and "The Jar" were published online in *Canadian Poetries* at www.canadianpoetries.com.

CATHERINE GREENWOOD'S poetry has been widely published in journals and anthologies, and has received several prizes, including a National Magazine Gold Award. Her first book, *The Pearl King and Other Poems*, was a Kiriyama Prize notable book. Her day jobs have ranged from working at a community services thrift store to teaching English literature at Qingdao University in China. At present she works for BC's Ministry of Justice in Victoria, where she lives with her husband, the writer Steve Noyes, and their cat Prudence.